The Virtuous Woman
A Study of the Proverbs 31 Woman

Tisha Carter
Theological Doctoral Candidate

Copyright 2015 by T. Carter (Tisha Linen-Carter)
© 2015

Published by Project 31 Ministries, LLC. 2018

All rights reserved. No part of this bible study may be reproduced in any form or by any electronic or mechanical means, including information storage and retrieval systems, without permission in writing from the author, except by a reviewer who may quote brief passages in a review.

All scripture quotations noted are taken from *YouVersion* published electronically by LifeChurch.tv Copyright 2015

Definitions are extracted from *Webster Dictionary App* published electronically by Merriam-Webster Inc. Copyright 2015 Apple Inc.

Commentary quotations noted are taken from *Matthew Henry's Concise Commentary* on the Whole Bible published by Thomas Nelson, Inc. Nashville Tennessee Copyright 1997, *New Illustrated Bible Commentary* published by Thomas Nelson, Inc. Nashville Tennessee 1999

Table of Contents

Curriculum Overview   4

Study Begins   6

Wrap It Up   63

Scripture Memory   65

CURRICULUM OVERVIEW

The Book of Proverbs is understood to be the guidebook in for Christian living when compared to the other books in the Bible. While the Bible itself, instructs believers on how to live for Christ, Proverbs is considered the most instructional book of them all. The Book of Proverbs offers a clear and concise code of conduct that offers believers a barometer for Christian living.

Therefore, the introduction of the Proverbs 31 woman, found in the book of instruction, implies her importance in the expectation of God towards Christian women. The Proverbs 31 woman is a blueprint for biblical womanhood. The virtues illustrated in Proverbs 31:10-31 communicate God's direct expectations for biblical womanhood. She is a Godly woman of influence. If there is a desire to earnestly seek a life pleasing to Christ, the Proverbs 31 woman provides an example for all women.

This bible study is designed to initiate, encourage, and empower women to live for Christ through the virtues of the Proverbs 31 woman that defines biblical womanhood. God's word provides a map to biblical womanhood through the Proverbs 31 woman.

The study goes through 20 weeks of dissecting each scripture to better understand the characteristics of each virtue. A reflection of the true meaning of each word creates an opportunity for self-examination and growth. The hope is to gain a more simplified explanation of the scriptures that are applicable to everyday living for Christ.

The weekly lessons begin with the scripture for the week. The scripture is then dissected through providing the definitions for the words that explains the virtues. Following the definitions will be a series of questions to initiate a more tangible understanding of how the virtues may affect the reader. After completing the questions there is an area for journaling to encourage self-reflection. After Lesson Nineteen there is a Wrap-up and scripture cards. The scriptures are flash cards of the passage to help with scriptures memory. Cut out the verse that is most relative for memorization.

This way of studying the scriptures is offered in an attempt to create an approach towards studying that enables a more analytical and relatable experience.

The devotional is most affective in small groups or classroom settings. Discussions of the questions and journal entries is very viable to the overall process of acquiring the virtues. Additionally, personal growth is easily measured in group settings.

The overall goal is to encourage women to exhibit the virtues of the Proverbs 31 woman in their everyday lives. Let's begin!

LESSON ONE

Proverbs 31:10
A woman of noble character who can find? She is worth far more than rubies

Definitions

noble – having and showing qualities such as honesty, generosity and courage; possessing excellence in characteristics and appearances.

character – moral excellence and firmness; qualities of nobility; lacking rudeness.

worth – to the fullest extent of one's value or ability; usefulness or importance

1. After reading the definitions listed above, what is your perception of the noble woman described in the scripture?

_____

_____

_____

_____

2. Do you feel you possess some of these qualities? If so, in what ways?

_____

_____

_____

_____

3. How do these areas influence your relationship with Christ?

_____

_____

_____

_____

4. Are there areas of your life where you may need to practice these qualities more?

_____

_____

_____

_____

5. What do you think God's expectations are of us with regards to this scripture?

_____

_____

_____

_____

Use the space below to reflect and journal any additional thoughts about Lesson One.

_____

_____

LESSON TWO

Proverbs 31:11-12
11 Her husband has full confidence in her and lacks nothing of value 12 She brings him good, not harm, all the days of her life.

Read: Proverbs 12:4, 18:22, 19:14; Isaiah 61:10; Matthew 25:1

Definitions

confidence – a feeling or belief that someone or something is good or has the ability to succeed at something; the consciousness of one's reliance; faith or belief.

value – usefulness and importance; trustworthy; intrinsically desirable

good – high quality; favorable character; suitable; presentable

1. As God is the bridegroom for every believer, what are His expectations for us as His bride?

_____

_____

_____

_____

2. Are you currently exhibiting the characteristics expressed in these verses? If so, how?

_____

_____

_____

_____

3. In what areas of your life can you improve with regards to the characteristics listed in these verses?

_____

_____

_____

_____

Complete this week with a journal entry.

_____

_____

_____

_____

_____

_____

_____

_____

_____

_____

_____

LESSON THREE

Proverbs 31:13-14
13 She seeks wool and flax, and willingly works with her hands. 14 She is like the merchant ships, she brings her food from afar.

Definitions

willingly – not refusing to do something; eager to help; relating to the will or power of choosing.

works – activity in which one exerts strength or faculties to do or perform something as a means of livelihood.

brings – to come with something; to bear as an attribute or characteristic (brings years of experience to the position).

1. What is your current attitude towards work? Are you currently working?

___

___

___

___

2. Read Proverbs 12:11 and Colossians 3:23. What is God's expectations towards us and working?

___

___

___

___

3. Are there aspects of your work that can improve based on the definitions and God's expectations?

_____
_____
_____
_____

4. How has your vocation of work impacted your relationship with Christ?

_____
_____
_____
_____

5. Take some time to journal about what you've learned about yourself this week as it applies to your attitude towards work and God's expectations of how Christians should work.

_____
_____
_____
_____
_____

LESSON FOUR

Proverbs 31:15-16
15 She also rises while it is yet night, and provides food for her household, and a portion for her maidservants. 16 She considers a field and buys it; From her profits she plants a vineyard.

Read: Exodus 19:5, Deuteronomy 11:1, Proverbs 13:4

Definitions
rises – to get up from sleep; upright position; to respond warmly

provides – to make available; to make a certain thing happen; give what is wanted or needed.

profits – the advantage or benefit that is gained from doing something

plants – to put or place; establish; settle

1. What are the requirements of the Proverbs 31 woman expressed in this passage?

___

___

___

___

2. What are God's expectations of us with regards to the behaviors explained in this passage?

___

___

___

___

3. Are you currently demonstrating these behaviors, if so how?

_____

_____

_____

_____

4. What did you draw from the supportive scriptures provided in this week's lesson?

_____

_____

_____

_____

5. Complete this week with a journal entry about what you have learned about yourself.

_____

_____

_____

_____

_____

_____

LESSON FIVE

Proverbs 31:17
17 She girds herself with strength; and strengthens her arms.

Read: Philippians 4:13, Psalm 119:11; Ephesians 6:10-18

Definitions
gird – to be equipped; prepared; encircled

strength – the ability to resist being moved, waivered, broken; capacity for endurance

strengthen – increase in value; more forceful; more effective

1. Where do you find your personal strength?

_____

_____

_____

_____

_____

2. From where does the Proverbs 31 gain her strength?

_____

_____

_____

_____

_____

3. What are God's expectations of us with regards to the behaviors explained in this passage?

_____

_____

_____

_____

4. Do you gird yourself with the word of God daily, if so how?

_____

_____

_____

_____

5. Take this time to journal about some scriptures that give you strength during the week.

_____

_____

_____

_____

_____

_____

_____

LESSON SIX

Proverbs 31:18
18 She perceives that her merchandise is good, her lamp does not go out by night.

Read: Colossians 3:23-24; 1 Corinthians 10:31

Definitions
perceives – be aware; having understanding; to notice

merchandise – goods; commodities; the occupation

good – to be equipped; prepared; encircled

1. What is your perception of the Proverbs 31 woman's goods based on the definitions above?

___

2. What are God's expectations of us with regards to this passage?

___

3. How do you perceive your own goods?

_____
_____
_____
_____

4. Use the lines below to journal about God's intentions towards your goods?

_____
_____
_____
_____
_____
_____
_____
_____

LESSON SEVEN

Proverbs 31:19
19 She stretches out her hands to the distaff, and her hand holds the spindle.

Read: Genesis 1:26-27; Timothy 3:11; Titus 2:3

Definitions
stretches – extension through positions; to reach out; to make more

distaff – woman's work or domain; the female branch of the family

holds – to have or keep; put in a specified position or place

1. What is the importance of this verse in the grand scheme of who the Proverbs 31 woman is?

_____
_____
_____
_____
_____

2. What places and positions is God asking you to hold or stretch?

_____
_____
_____
_____
_____

3. What tactics are you using to complete God's request?

___

4. Take time to journal what Proverbs 31:19 and the supporting verses communicate you? How do they influence your relationship with Christ?

___

LESSON EIGHT

Proverbs 31:20
20 She extends her hand to the poor, yes, she reaches out her hands to the needy.

Read: Deuteronomy 14:28, 15:8; Proverbs 19:17; Luke 4:23

Definitions
extends – be aware; having understand; to continue

reaches – to move or stretch out; to extend; to arrive

poor – having few possessions; only having enough for basic needs; lacking

1. What are your thoughts on Proverbs 31:20?

_____

_____

_____

_____

2. What do you think are God's expectations based on this verse and the definitions listed?

_____

_____

_____

3. How have you been charitable? How will you be charitable in the future?

_____
_____
_____
_____
_____

4. Use the space below to journal about God's expectations about being charitable

_____
_____
_____
_____
_____
_____
_____
_____
_____
_____

LESSON NINE

Proverbs 31:21
21 She is not afraid of snow for her household. For all her household is clothed with scarlet.

Read: Isaiah 41:10; Philippians 4:6-7; Habakkuk 2:2

Definitions
afraid – filled with fear; apprehension; full of concern or regret; having strong dislike of hard work

clothed – to provide; to cover; enhance significantly

1. Why does the Proverbs 31 woman not afraid?

_____
_____
_____
_____

2. What does the supporting scriptures have to do with being afraid?

_____
_____
_____
_____

3. What areas of your life do you feel the most fear?

_____
_____

4. How do you deal with fear?

_____
_____
_____
_____
_____
_____
_____

5. Use the lines below to journal about how fear impacts your relationship with Christ.

_____
_____
_____
_____
_____
_____
_____

LESSON TEN

Proverbs 31:22
22 She makes tapestry for herself; Her clothing is fine linen and purple.

Read: 1 Corinthians 3:16-17; Psalm 139:14; 1 Peter 2:9

Definitions
tapestry – complexity of richness of design; heavy textile; complicated textile

fine – free from impurity; pure; very good; delicate, subtle, sensitive; superior in quality; elegant

1. What does this verse communicate about the Proverbs 31 woman?

___

2. What are God's expectations of her with regards to herself?

___

3. How does this verse impact your relationship with Christ?

   _____

   _____

   _____

   _____

   _____

   _____

4. Use the lines below to journal how the verses for this week impact your daily life? What does it mean to you as a Christian woman?

   _____

   _____

   _____

   _____

   _____

   _____

   _____

   _____

LESSON ELEVEN

Proverbs 31:23
23 Her husband is known in the gates, when he sits among the elders of the land.

Read: 2 Corinthians 5:20; Ephesians 5:1-20

Definitions
known – generally accepted as something specified; familiar; generally recognized

among – in or through; in the presence of; in the midst

1. Why does the Proverbs 31 woman represent in this passage?

_____

_____

_____

_____

_____

2. What are God's expectations?

_____

_____

_____

_____

_____

3. Does your life communicate to others that you are a Christian? If so, how?

_____
_____
_____
_____
_____

4. The Proverbs 31 woman is guarding her husband's reputation. Are you guarding God's reputation? If so, how?

_____
_____
_____
_____
_____

5. Complete this week's lesson by journaling your thoughts about the verses discussed this week.

_____
_____
_____
_____

LESSON TWELVE

Proverbs 31:24
24 She makes linen garments and sells them; and supplies sashes for the merchants.

Read: Romans 12:1-2; Matthew 5:16; Luke 3:10-11

Definitions
makes – to build, create, or produce; to cause to exist; to intend

supplies – to provide; to add; make available

1. Why do you think the Proverbs 31 woman supplies sashes for the merchants?

___

___

___

___

2. What is God's expectations of us with regard to this passage?

___

___

___

___

3. How can you apply these attributes to your life?

_____
_____
_____
_____

4. What areas of your life currently display these attributes?

_____
_____
_____
_____

5. Take this time to journal your thoughts about the verses discussed in this week's lessons.

_____
_____
_____
_____
_____
_____

LESSON THIRTEEN

Proverbs 31:25
25 Strength and honor are her clothing; she shall rejoice in time to come.

Read: 2 Corinthians 5:20; Ephesians 2:10, 4:1-3; 2 Chronicles 7:14

Definitions
strength – the ability to resist being moved; determined and effective; resisting attack; solidity; potency of effect

honor – showing merited respect; one who's works bring respect; a good name; high moral standards and behaviors

rejoice – great delight; given joy; expressing happiness

1. What are characteristics of honor?

_____

_____

_____

_____

_____

2. How can we honor God with our lives?

_____

_____

_____

_____

_____

3. How does the contents of these verses impact your relationship with Christ?

_____

_____

_____

_____

_____

4. Do you delight in honoring God? If so, how?

_____

_____

_____

_____

_____

5. Use the lines below to journal your thoughts about this week's lesson.

_____

_____

_____

_____

_____

LESSON FOURTEEN

Proverbs 31:26
26 She opens her mouth with wisdom, and on her tongue is the law of kindness.

Read: 1 Peter 3:10; Colossians 4:6; Ephesians 4:49; Proverbs 10:19, 15:4

Definitions
mouth – a natural opening that passes things into the body

tongue – a particular way or quality of speaking; manner or quality of utterance with respect to tone or sound; a sense of what is expressed.

wisdom – knowledge of that is proper and reasonable; good sense of judgment; natural ability to understand; discernment of inner qualities

kindness – the quality or state of being kind; benevolence; grace; mercy' favor

1. How does the Proverbs 31 woman speak?

_____

_____

_____

_____

2. How does God want us to speak?

_____

_____

_____

_____

3. What is required of us according to this verse?

_____

_____

_____

_____

_____

4. How does speaking with wisdom impact your relationship with God?

_____

_____

_____

_____

_____

5. Use the space below to journal about the areas in which you may struggle with speaking according to the scriptures. Detail an action plan address these areas.

_____

_____

_____

_____

_____

LESSON FIFTEEN

Proverbs 31:27
27 She watches over the ways of household; and does not eat the bread of idleness.

Read: Habakkuk 2:2; Psalm 90:12; Proverbs 16:9

Definitions
watches – to give your attention to a situation; to look at for an amount of time; to be attentive; vigilant

eat – to consume; to bear the expense of; take a loss

idleness – not working; not occupied; lazy; shiftless

1. What is God's main focus for the Proverbs 31 woman in this verse?

___

2. What are God's expectations of us based on this verse?

___

3. How do you manage your time?

_____

_____

_____

_____

_____

_____

4. How does managing your time impact your relationship with God?

_____

_____

_____

_____

5. Use the lines below to devise a plan to manage your time according to the expectations of God communicated in the verses from this week's lesson.

_____

_____

_____

_____

_____

LESSON SIXTEEN

Proverbs 31:28
28 Her children rise up and call her blessed; her husband also, and he praises her

Read: Deuteronomy 30:16; Proverbs 16:3; 1 Kings 2:3-4; Exodus 19:5

Definitions
up – a high position or place; higher ground; with greater intensity

blessed – honored; enjoying bliss; connected with God

praise – to express favorable judgment; glorify; celebrate attribution of perfections

1. What is the importance of this verse?
_____
_____
_____
_____
_____

2. What are God's expectations of us based on this verse?
_____
_____
_____
_____

3. How would the closest people in your life describe you?

_____
_____
_____
_____
_____
_____

4. What are the benefits of obedience to God?

_____
_____
_____
_____

5. Take this time to journal about how these verses influence your relationship with others and Christ.

_____
_____
_____
_____
_____

LESSON SEVENTEEN

Proverbs 31:29
29 Many daughters have done well, but you excel them all

Read: Philippians 4:8-9; Daniel 6:3; Colossians 3:23

Definitions
done – socially acceptable; sufficient; arrived

well – able-bodied; adequate; tolerable; whole

excel – superior; surpassing others; accomplished

1. How do you feel when something is done well?
___
___
___
___

2. How do you think God feels when we have done well?
___
___
___
___

3. What do you aspire to do well daily?

_____
_____
_____
_____
_____
_____
_____

4. In what areas are you challenged to do well?

_____
_____
_____
_____
_____

5. Use this area to journal about what revelations you may have had during this week's lesson.

_____
_____
_____
_____

LESSON EIGHTEEN

Proverbs 31:30
30 Charm is deceitful, and beauty is passing, but a woman who fears the Lord, she shall be praised.

Read: Proverbs 1:7; Romans 5:1-5; Psalm 31:29; Proverbs 22:4, 28:14

Definitions
deceitful – not honest; misleading; deceptive

beauty – graceful; ornamental; excellent quality

passing – moving beyond something

1. What kind of beauty is God referencing in this passage?
_____
_____
_____
_____
_____

2. How important is your outward appearance to you?
_____
_____
_____
_____
_____

3. How relevant is your inward beauty?

_____

_____

_____

_____

4. How can you apply the aspects of this verse to your life?

_____

_____

_____

_____

5. Take some time to journal about how these week's verses have impacted your life and your relationship with Christ.

_____

_____

_____

_____

LESSON NINETEEN

Proverbs 31:31
31 Give her of the fruit of her hands, and let her own works praise her in the gates.

Read: Galatians 5:22-23; Matthew 7:19-20; James 2:17,26

Definitions
give – to put into the possession of another; to transfer; yield to another

fruit – a result or reward; a state of bearing

works – a specific task; activity; physical effort

1. What are the fruits of the spirit?
___
___
___
___
___

2. Which fruits of the spirit are most prevalent in the Proverbs 31 verses?
___
___
___
___

3. Are you bearing good fruit? If so, how? If not, why?

___

___

___

___

___

___

4. Which fruits are most challenging for you?

___

___

___

___

___

___

5. Use the area below to journal about this week's lesson.

___

___

___

___

___

___

WRAP IT UP

Now that we have completed the study, let's take some time to assess what we gained:

1. Do you see a common overall thread of any characteristics you excel in?
_____
_____
_____
_____

2. Do you see a common overall thread of any characteristics you may need to improve?
_____
_____
_____
_____

3. What characteristics of the Proverbs 31 woman can you most relate to?
_____
_____
_____
_____

4. Which characteristics of the Proverbs 31 woman do you find most challenging?
_____
_____
_____
_____

5. What have you learned about God through this study?
_____
_____
_____
_____

6. What have you learned about your relationship with God through this study?
_____
_____
_____
_____

7. Do you feel enriched spiritually by the experience and the process?
_____
_____
_____
_____

SCRIPTURE MEMORY

31:10 Who can find a virtuous wife? For her worth is far Above rubies	*31:11* The heart of her husband Safely trusts her; So he will have no lack of gain
31:12 She does him good not evil All the days of her life	*31:13* She seeks wool and flax, And willingly works with her Hands.
31:14 She is like the merchant ships, She brings her food from afar.	*31:15* She also rises while it is yet night, And provides food for her household And portion for her maidservants
31:16 She considers a field and buys it; From her profits she plants vineyards.	*31:17* She girds herself with strength And strengthens her arms.

31:18 She perceives that her merchandise is good, And her lamp does not go out By night.	**31:19** She stretches out her hands to the Distaff. And her hand holds the spindle.
31:20 She extends her hand to the poor, Yes, she reaches out her hands to the needy	**31:21** She is not afraid of the snow For her household, For all her household is clothed with scarlet
31:22 She makes tapestry for herself; Her clothing is fine linen and purple	**31:23** Her husband is known in the gates, When he sits among the elders of the land.
31:24 She makes linen garments and sells them, And supplies sashes for the merchants	**31:25** Strength and honor are her clothing; She shall rejoice in time to come.
31:26 She opens her mouth with wisdom, And on her tongue is the law of kindness	**31:27** She watches over the ways of her household, And does not eat the bread of idleness.

31:28 *Her children rise up and call her blessed;* *Her husband also, and he praises her;*	*31:29* *Many daughters have done well,* *But you excel them all..*
31:30 *Charms is deceitful and beauty is passing, But a woman who fears the Lord, she shall be praised.*	*31:31* *Give her of the fruit of her hands, And let her own works praise her in the gates*

Made in the USA
Lexington, KY
28 February 2018